A gift for:

Mikeesa LeAnn

From:

Your loving mother ☺

July 2, 2009

glimmers of
grace

Sparkling Reminders to Encourage You

A Women of Faith® Gift Book

Designed by The Propel Group, Dallas, Texas.
www.propelgroup.com

ISBN
13: 978-1-4041-0478-5
10: 1-4041-0478-X

www.thomasnelson.com
www.womenoffaith.com

Printed and bound in China.

Contents

The Gift of Grace

Grace in the Daily Grind

Hearts that Glimmer with Grace

Grace Under Pressure

God's Great Grace

Acknowledgements

The life of grace
and the love of
Christ are nothing if
not extravagant.

—*Eugene Peterson*

THE GIFT OF GRACE

GRACE

ELEGANCE
charm
loveliness
kindness
benevolence
COMPASSION
mercy

sympathy
courtesy

graciousness
forgiveness

A Gracious Kindness

In the bank the other day, a woman came
in with a tiny baby and a toddler. She walked
to the end of a long line where we had been
waiting for 30 minutes for our turn with
a teller. Just as the gentleman in front of
me reached the head of the line, he motioned
for the mother with the children to take
his place, as he smilingly went back to
where she had been standing and took hers.
He never said a word, but was suddenly
everybody's hero.

Life in Christ permits us to accept and love
others just as they are, no matter their status,
color, race, religion, creed, or circumstances.
Not only that, but it encourages us to
serve people we don't even know. When
this happens, we manifest loving kindness
toward others.

Luci Swindoll
Women of Faith Devotional Bible

3

*Let the words
of my mouth
and the meditation of my heart
be acceptable in Your sight, O LORD,
my strength and
my Redeemer.*

Psalm 19:14

Goodwill and Grace

I love words! In the night they accumulate inside of me, and then at daybreak I split open like an overripe watermelon spewing words like seeds. It is said that women have more words and a greater need to speak them than men. Yet I've met many sedate women; in fact, I collect quiet friends for obvious reasons.

So imagine when I stumbled on Psalm 19:14 and realized the words I speak should be acceptable to the Lord. Acceptable? In the Hebrew *acceptable* means "full of favor, kindness, goodwill, and grace." Hmm…that edited my utterances dramatically. I'd been given to bouts of nitpicking, sporadic sessions of whining, and spouts of vanity. Conversationally, I was at least three quarts low on grace.

With the Lord's help, I have given up my endless verbiage (generally) and weigh my words more carefully (usually).

Patsy Clairmont
Women of Faith Devotional Bible

Be kind to one
another, tenderhearted,
forgiving one another,
even as God in Christ
forgave you.

Ephesians 4:32

Kindness and Tenderness

Here's an exercise: Each morning when you wake up, check the fertile soil of your heart to see if any bitter seed has taken root. That friend who betrayed you, the boss who berated you, the husband who barely understands you—bitter seeds will try to take root in every garden. Weeds are like that.

Next do this: For every bitter root that's come up, apply the greatest weed killer of all—forgiveness. To forgive is to cultivate a garden God will delight in, one filled with the flowers of kindness and tenderness.

Karen Kingsbury
Women of Faith Devotional Bible

You will never be called upon to
give anyone more grace than God
has already given you.

—Max Lucado

Honey-Sweet Grace

I'm fascinated by bumblebees and also by their cousins, the honeybees. In *The Bee Book*, writer Daphne More explains that the bee's stinger is barbed, and when the bee thrusts the stinger into "human skin the bee cannot withdraw it. It twirls about until it tears itself free, leaving behind the sting and parts of its body. The injury is always fatal to the bee."

When I read that fact, I thought how it resembles what happens to us when we respond angrily and hurtfully to those who have wronged us. We *can* hurt them back. We can sting them with angry words and hurtful actions. But in the end, we probably do more damage to ourselves than we inflict upon them, especially when we consider whether or not our behavior was Christlike. What sadness we feel when we realize once again that we have failed to measure up. We bow our heads and ask the Savior to do for us what we've been unable to do for others: forgive us.

And once again He extends His honey-sweet gift of grace to us—and urges us to share it.

Thelma Wells
Listen Up, Honey

Jesus brings together our heads and our
hearts to make us persons who reflect
the harmony of grace and truth.

—Luci Swindoll

Grace to Forgive

Many of us would rather hang on to resentment than forgive. We know forgiving will get rid of the resentment that is weighing us down, but even that is not sufficient motivation. The sobering truth about hanging on to the resentment is that we create for ourselves an interior concentration camp. In that camp we sit behind the bars of our anger, our resentment, and our bitterness.... We rationalize…saying they don't deserve to be forgiven.

Though "they" may not deserve forgiveness, may I suggest that neither do you deserve the consequences that come with a lack of forgiveness. It was bad enough to be hurt the first time, but it is inexcusable to find yourself imprisoned in the concentration camp for something you did not deserve.

Forgiving those who do not deserve forgiveness does not mean that what they did was right. Forgiveness does not grant approval. Neither does forgiveness grant them access to you and your life. Forgiveness simply sets you free.

Marilyn Meberg
The Zippered Heart

Offer your words like gifts that, when unwrapped, bring grace to the hearer.

—Patsy Clairmont

Celebrate Someone!

Nothing is more important than words. In fact,
my favorite invention on earth is the alphabet.
Where would we be without it? Don't hesitate to
say words that build up and strengthen someone.
Applaud others with kind words. And put them in
writing to be kept and cherished.

**If you want to make someone happy, figure out how
to say thank you in a fresh, loving way.**

- Send a card.

- Write a warm, tender e-mail.

- Communicate the good news instead of the bad.

- Mail a postcard or a letter.

- Send someone you love a detailed description of
everything going on in the neighborhood.

- Tell someone what you love and miss about them.

- Celebrate someone!

Luci Swindoll
Contagious Joy

Mercy is an act of kindness.
It is also an expression
of tenderness.

—R. C. Sproul

A Caring Compassion

The account of Jesus' life in the four gospels gives us the answer to His amazing power with people. Repeatedly the text reads, "He looked at [her] with eyes of compassion." Within a verse or two, something else becomes apparent: "He touched them." Everywhere Jesus went He did those two things.

1. *He looked at people, showing He really cared about them.* Compassion always makes me feel like people are concerned about my feelings, emotional responses, and hurts. Instead of feeling threatened, I feel valued and loved. Usually that feeling comes nonverbally from someone before he or she speaks a word.

2. *He touched people.* The woman who touches others with a warm greeting or affirming pat appears much more approachable and is perceived as a person of warmth. Intimidation is not present. Fears begin to melt away.

Carol Kent
Tame Your Fears

Loving Ourselves

So often we don't like who we are. We don't
like what we see in the mirror, we're dissatisfied
with how we look or what we weigh, or we're
disappointed in how we've misbehaved or how we've
treated someone else. And the sum total of that
prevents us from truly loving ourselves.

At one time or another I've felt unlovable for all the
reasons listed above, and I imagine you have too.
And on rare occasions, I still do. But I've learned
that God loves me, no matter what. As long as I am
confident in God's love for me, I eventually come
around to the realization that I can love me too.

What happens when I love me unconditionally?
Well, I'm more content, I feel appreciated, I'm
sweeter to other people, I don't get my feelings hurt
because I'm secure inside, and I do things for other
people without expecting something from them in
return—all those things and more. In short, I do
unto others what I want done unto me!

Luci Swindoll
Life! Celebrate It

Your parents may have given you genes, but God gives you grace.

Your parents may be responsible for your body, but God has taken charge of your soul.

You may get your looks from your mother, but you get eternity from your Father, your heavenly Father.

—Max Lucado

God knows the whole story
of your life because He is the
Author of your biography.
He knows the last chapter, and
He thinks you are wonderful.

—Jan Silvious

*God is able to
make all grace
abound toward
you,
that you…
may have an
abundance
for every good
work.*

2 Corinthians 9:8

Grace Is a Wide Space

I'm so grateful Jesus enables me to change, one groaning effort at a time, and I'm thankful for those folks in my life who have given me the space and time to change. It's easy (but not loving) to view a person in one light and mentally lock that person into never being different. When that happens, even if the individual changes, she might feel bound to her old behavior when in our predetermined presence.

Grace is a liberating quality—no, let me restate that. Grace is a required quality for family members, mates, moms, servants, and friends. Grace is a wide space, acreage full of forgiveness, humility, acceptance, safety, and love. When I consider what great things the Lord has done for me, grace and friendships make me want to break out bags of confetti, kazoos, and my most outrageous party hat!

Patsy Clairmont
The Hat Box

What things are you thankful for?

_____

_____

_____

_____

_____

_____

_____

_____

Thankful!

If you were to make a list of all the things you are thankful for, what would they be? Would they be health, strength, stamina, hope, happiness, or a heart of love? …What about learning, and laughter?

Given the time and space, I could add about a hundred thousand things for which to be grateful. On my list, however, I would include people, books, references, Internet, e-mail, coworkers, family, friends, and enemies (they encourage me to pray). And I can't forget my bags of pantyhose with the runs in them that I wear under my trousers (they are soooo necessary).

If we had the full 168 hours in a week to speak and sing praises to God for what He has done for us, we wouldn't be able to complete them, because as soon as we finish praising Him for one thing, He gives us something else.

Now, that's just like God.

Thelma Wells
Contagious Joy

GRACE IN THE DAILY GRIND

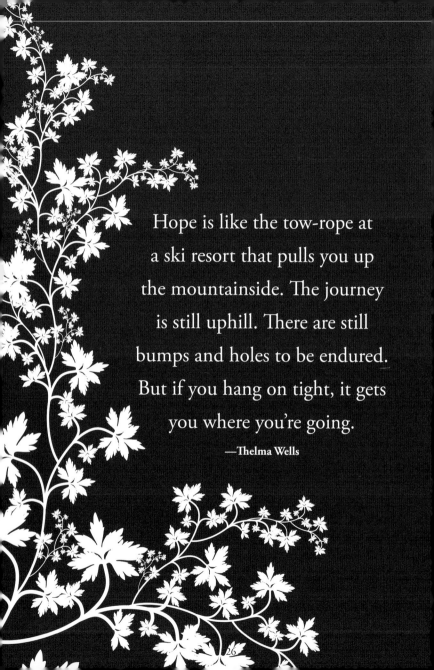

Hope is like the tow-rope at
a ski resort that pulls you up
the mountainside. The journey
is still uphill. There are still
bumps and holes to be endured.
But if you hang on tight, it gets
you where you're going.

—Thelma Wells

Glistening Hope

I've been studying about hope…the Hope Diamond, that is.
Did you know that the Hope Diamond started off at more
than 112 carats, but today it's just over 45 carats? Talk about
broken. Wouldn't you love to have a chip off that block?

Now, when I say only 45 carats, that's compared to its
original size, which is, shall we say, outside of my grocery
budget. Why, I have a friend with a five-carat diamond ring,
and she needs help just to tote her hand around. I've offered
to literally take it off her hands, but so far, no deal. And I
thought it such a friendly gesture!

I sometimes wish I could wear my hope as a pendant
so all who see it might be drawn to my dazzling Christ.
But isn't that what happens when we live out our faith in
spite of hardships and opposition? What looks impossible
suddenly glistens with hope, and others come to
observe and ask questions.

Ever notice how a dark velvet backdrop enhances
a diamond's qualities? So, too, does hope shine on a
backdrop of pain, failure, and loss.

Patsy Clairmont
All Cracked Up

Deliberately choose to look for joy
in every step of your journey through life
and to share it with others.

—Barbara Johnson

28

Find the Giggle

I love to laugh. I believe a giggle is always loitering about even in the most devastating of circumstances. I make a point of shuffling through the rubble in search of that giggle.

This isn't denial. I need to feel and express my pain. But I also need to find the light side— and there is *always* a light side! I've noticed that when I laugh about some minor part of a problem or controversy or worry, the whole situation suddenly seems much less negative to me. After a good laugh, I can then rethink my circumstances. As a result, that which was threatening may now seem less threatening.

Marilyn Meberg
I'd Rather Be Laughing

Everyday Acts of Kindness

Noah surely felt strengthened as he walked with God and lived in His favor. How else could he have started such an outrageous project as building a huge boat in a desert nation where it seldom rained—when he was six hundred years old? Imagine the teasing Noah must have gotten from his friends as he carefully cut and assembled the gopherwood. Picture the old man struggling to coat the giant vessel inside and out with tar while his neighbors stood around the ladder, laughing and criticizing him. And then picture God holding the ladder steady and shouting up encouragement only Noah could hear: "That's it, Noah. You're getting it. Oops. That's okay. Good job, son!"

In the same way, God's grace empowers us to do everyday acts of kindness and outrageous acts of courage on His behalf. Step out confidently on the path God sets before you, no matter how outrageous the goal may seem at the time. The God who steadied the ladder for Noah will hold you steady as you do His work today.

Barbara Johnson
Women of Faith Devotional Bible

Grace means it's not about what we can do, but about what God does because of His love for us.

—Marilyn Meberg

Grace and Truth

Time is God's way of bringing about the wholeness lost in Eden. It takes time to work the soil with his ingredients of grace and truth, and to allow them to take effect....

We will encounter problems if we do not realize that a Christian goes through different stages of growth. We must mature in one stage before we can go on to the next. To progress to that next stage, we must have time along with grace and truth.... An apple tree needs time to mature before its limbs can carry the weight of a ripe fruit. God understands such a developmental process; He invented it. He uses time.

Dr. Henry Cloud
Changes that Heal

When the Spiritual Meter Points to Low

I get asked a lot, "What do you do when you don't feel funny?"
All I can tell them is that I just go [on stage] and do [my comedy
routine]. If I waited until I felt funny, some days I might not
even get out of bed. When I don't feel funny, I just *be* funny.
Pardon my grammar. But if I can just do that, then most likely
that funny feeling will come loping in sometime before the night
is over—late, yes, but at least it shows up.

And you know what else? Sometimes I don't feel very spiritual either. I mean, who does feel like they're sitting in heaven's great room 24–7? We're human. We feel tired, we feel beat up, we feel lonely, left, betrayed, empty, and weary. On those kinds of days, feeling spiritual seems like an ancient memory....

So what do I do when the spiritual meter points to the low end? Same thing as with the funny: I just *do*. I listen to praise music, I sing praise music, I read my Joyce Myers and Beth Moore books, I read my Bibles.... If I depend on emotion, emotion will let me down. So I do what I know. And the funny thing about feeling spiritual is that if you just do what you know, just *be* spiritual, eventually that feeling will return, will come loping in.

Chonda Pierce
Roadkill on the Highway to Heaven

Deposit only positive
thoughts in your mind.
Withdraw only positive
thoughts from your mind.

—Anonymous

A Well-Balanced Life

What do we do with our expectations?
We manage them. In some cases, they need
to be lowered. In other cases, they need to
be raised. We need to zero in on reality and
choose to live within realistic parameters.
So often our expectations are not only out
of balance in the marriage relationship, but
they're also out of balance with our kids.
We want the best for them. Actually, we want
perfection for them. That is not a realistic
expectation. We cannot provide perfection,
and they cannot deliver it. So we lower our
expectations and accept the fact that the kids
next door have the flu and your four-year-old
just spent the afternoon at their house.

Managing our expectations has nothing
whatever to do with negative thinking. It has
everything to do with realistic thinking.

Marilyn Meberg
Since You Asked

37

May your day be fashioned with joy,

sprinkled with dreams,

and touched by the miracle of love.

—Barbara Johnson

Laugh Lines from Barbara Johnson:

• The only time a woman wishes she were a year older is when she is expecting a baby.

• The second day of a diet is always easier than the first. By the second day you're off it.

• A woman marries a man expecting he will change, but he doesn't. A man marries a woman expecting that she won't change, and she does.

• Hospitality is making your guests feel at home even though you wish they were!

• The best way to forget your troubles is to wear tight shoes.

• There are two times when a man doesn't understand a woman—before marriage and after marriage.

If you have the Shepherd, you have grace for every sin, direction for every turn, a candle for every corner, and an anchor for every storm. You have everything you need.

—Max Lucado

Always Grace

If you are married, chances are, your marriage isn't perfect. I'm pretty confident about that because marriage involves two imperfect people. My husband, Barry, and I love each other deeply,…but I am not everything Barry needs just as he is not everything I need….

But here is what makes our marriage a joy to both of us: we are learning that everything we need we find in God alone, and we get to bring those gifts to one another. If my attitude toward Barry on any given day is based on how he is feeling, we are on very shaky ground. He might be having a great day and feel warm and affectionate, which might motivate me to be sweet and kind. But he might be having a bad day, where he just wants to be left alone for a while. If I am looking to him for how I should respond, I'm setting us both up for disaster.

On the other hand, if I understand that God *always* loves me, *always* watches over me, *always* has grace and mercy for me, *always* offers peace and joy, then I have a full heart that can share warmth and affection.

Sheila Walsh
Extraordinary Faith

If we trust in the
sovereignty of God,
we wrestle our way
to peace in the
knowledge that if an
answer to prayer is for
our highest good, the
God who loves us will
not withhold it.

—Lana Bateman

A Channel for Grace

However uncertain I am about the way prayer
changes the unfolding of events, I have been
shown clearly that prayer changes *me*. When
I begin to pray for an enemy, my heart like
a fist clenched with anger, I am opened up
until I can no longer hold the resentment and
frustration. When I plead with the publican,
"Lord, have mercy on me, a sinner," I travel
a little deeper into the mercy of God. When
I confess with the father who cried out,
"I believe, help my unbelief," my faith is made
a little stronger.

Sometimes, when I offer up a prayer of
intercession for someone else, I discover that
in some mysterious way God actually uses my
prayer as a channel for His grace.

Carolyn Arends
Living the Questions

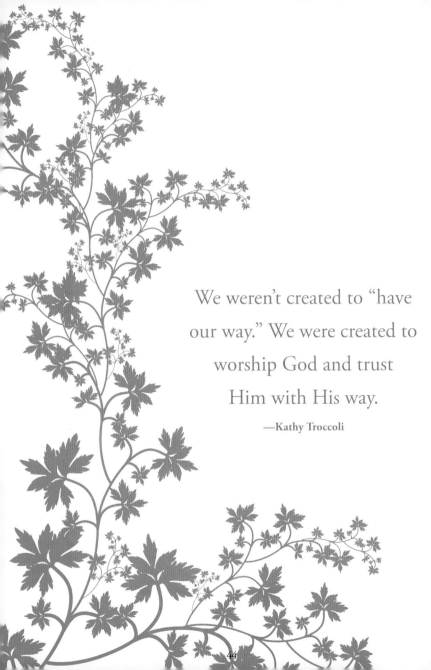

We weren't created to "have our way." We were created to worship God and trust Him with His way.

—**Kathy Troccoli**

Under God's Mercy

Here is the *really* liberating truth: Everything is not going to get fixed and healed in this lifetime—that's what Heaven is for. You have to decide what can go under the mercy of God (not to be confused with "under the rug"—because when stuff is swept under the rug, it always sneaks back out and eventually makes a gargantuan mountain that you can't navigate around). Under the mercy of God is a place where you put things when you know that they are not going to be healed in this lifetime. These are the things you can't fix in [other people] and they just need mercy. Grace. Forgiveness. And that is a perfectly okay place to start building something new—on the platform of mercy, forgiveness, and grace....

We all have "junk in the trunk"—the baggage and hurt that accompanies living. Your choice is whether you will put it up in the front seat, ask God to help you deal with it, allow Him to heal you from it, release it, and even laugh about it...or leave it in the trunk to rot and make you sick.

Anita Renfroe
If It's Not One Thing It's Your Mother

HEARTS THAT
GLIMMER WITH GRACE

"I will set my eyes on them for good…
I will give them a heart to know Me."

Jeremiah 24:6–7

A Grace-Filled Woman

I want to become the full-grown, fully mature, grace-filled
woman that God envisioned before I was even born.

I want to be the full-size, grown-up version of
that wonder-filled baby girl He knit together in
my mother's womb.

I want to be so in tune with Him and His thoughts and
ideas for me that I can know and celebrate on a daily basis
that I am fearfully and wonderfully made.

I want His dream for me to be a reality....

This great God of ours works in us to make us all we can
be. He does not just sit on the sidelines waiting for us to
trip up while we try to be a bigger girl than we are. He just
longs for us to grow and live each season of our lives to the
max, and He empowers us to do it if we really want to.

That's what being a Big Girl is all about: living life to the
fullest in all ways, in all places, and in all situations.

Jan Silvious
Big Girls Don't Whine

Friendly

HOSPITABLE
affectionate
loving
approachable
amiable
PLEASANT
kind
warmhearted
gracious
courteous
reliable
HELPFUL
generous

Girlfriend Attributes

Regardless of your age you've probably run into people issues. Mine began in infancy when I bellowed for attention and folks didn't immediately sprint to my cradle. Know what I mean? Left to our humanity, we tend to be self-serving in how we relate and what we expect from others.

I'm thankful that Jesus set a new standard for relationships when He showed Himself to be a servant and a friend. Servanthood and friendship are excellent handholding, girlfriend attributes. It's hard to separate the two when one is longing for and working toward healthy relationships, whether that be mother-child, husband-wife, or employee-boss.

Patsy Clairmont
The Hat Box

Grace and Care and Love

Mother told me once when I wanted to give
up on a friendship that wasn't going my way
to look at it from the other person's point of
view. She said something like, "You can't make
people into what you want them to be. People
are themselves. They're cut out of their own
cloth. Try to think about what you can give
them, not what they can give you."
That was good advice....

True friendships are characterized by grace,
truth, forgiveness, unselfishness, boundaries,
care and love in gigantic and mutual
proportion. Although they require hard work
and consistency from each party, we enjoy the
best of the best in life because when friends
come alongside, more light is added to our
path. Two are better than one! We lay down
our lives for our friends, they lay down their
lives for us, and in the end we all find true life.

Luci Swindoll
I Married Adventure

Because of God's grace and faithfulness to me, I can laugh at myself. I used to have such a fragile core that I felt diminished by any flaw that showed. Now I understand that I am indeed flawed, but I am redeemed and loved by God.

—Sheila Walsh

Our Best Features

I love the fact that Jesus chose the salty apostle
Peter—a guy whose big mouth got him into
all kinds of trouble his whole life—as the
cornerstone of His church, confident that
the mysterious machinations of grace would
transform Peter's tendency to blurt things out
into a great gift for proclaiming the truth....

We expect a God of power to obliterate our
weaknesses—instead we are more likely to
encounter a God of love who finds impossibly
creative ways to convert those liabilities into
our best features. Only the Author of love
could come up with a plot twist like this in
the story of redemption——we actually become
better not in spite of, but *because of*,
our infirmities.

Carolyn Arends
Living the Questions

God was thinking about us
when there was only form and
void in the world.
And He has never stopped
thinking about us.

—Thelma Wells

Loved Unconditionally

God made every intricate part of our beings,
like a master weaver who takes the finest
silk threads and makes a priceless garment
with precision, excellence, and exquisitely
great taste. The recipient of the garment
has the ability to accept this unique
treasure with dignity.

Yes, that's who you are. You are a creation
of God, made with His character, crafted with
His DNA, and loved unconditionally by
Him. God never makes junk!

Thelma Wells
Women of Faith Devotional Bible

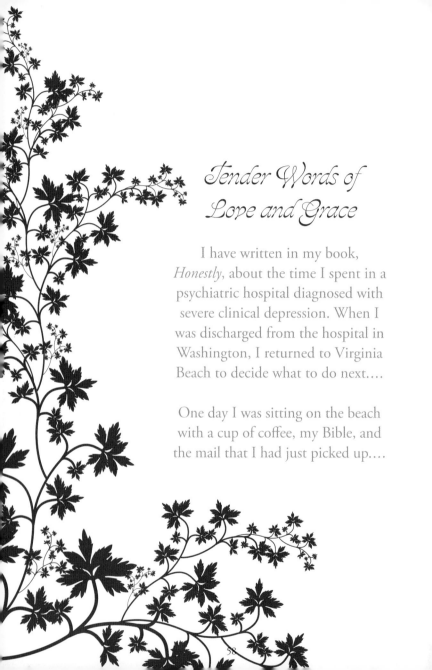

Tender Words of Love and Grace

I have written in my book, *Honestly*, about the time I spent in a psychiatric hospital diagnosed with severe clinical depression. When I was discharged from the hospital in Washington, I returned to Virginia Beach to decide what to do next....

One day I was sitting on the beach with a cup of coffee, my Bible, and the mail that I had just picked up....

I looked at my mail and saw a padded envelope that had a familiar address at the top—Ruth Graham [wife of Billy Graham]. My heart sank. I thought, *Oh no, Ruth has heard what happened to me. She is writing to tell me she is shocked…. Perhaps she wishes that she had not allowed me to film the shows with her.*

I opened the envelope and took out a little book, *Streams in the Desert*. Ruth had inscribed the most loving, tender words of grace and mercy and assured me of her prayers during that time. I soaked the book with my tears. I wept and wept. It seemed too good to be true. It wasn't just that Ruth had reached out with love and grace, but I heard a stronger voice speaking through this dear friend. I heard God say, *I am with you; I will never leave you.*

Sheila Walsh
Extraordinary Faith

When we are caught up in the
celebration of God there is
no room for negative living.

—Luci Swindoll

Playful People

Playful people look at life through a kaleidoscopic lens,
seeing all kinds of ways to find adventure and have fun.
They've unlocked the door to the child within—the muse
for our creativity. Here are a half dozen tips that may
help bring your muse into the sunlight:

- Figure out what the child within you wants
to do and do it.

- Listen to that tiny, soft voice inside and believe it.

- Quit conforming to what the world demands.

- Surround yourself with people who love
you and enjoy them.

- Create a life for yourself that's meaningful and live there.

- Keep in mind that imagination is more
important than knowledge.

Don't be afraid to explore playful pleasures in your life.
Let them spill outside the bounds of your leisure and work,
your home and office, your school and church.
Let them permeate your life.

Luci Swindoll
The Great Adventure

Glimmers in the Dark

When you were a child holding a mirror in
your hand, if you caught a glint of the sun,
that mirror reflected a beam that
could actually illumine a dark place.
That was pretty exciting! You had the
power to shine in the darkness. It was better
than holding a flashlight because the reflection
source was from above you, not from
batteries in your hand. It was supernatural
phenomena to every child.

Each of God's children has the power to
illumine the darkness. This light shows up in
different forms: humor, kindness, peace, hope,
grace—all characteristics that can come out of
us when the light Source shines through us.

Luci Swindoll
Women of Faith Devotional Bible

Be Who You Are

There is no one else in the whole wide world like you. I'm sure you have heard that before, but I wonder if you understand how true it is and how precious you are to God. We are not always treasured on this earth. Our relationships with our parents or friends or spouses can lead us to believe that we may be unique, but that it's not a good thing. So often we are encouraged to blend in, don't rock the boat, don't be different; but I say, rock that boat, and be who you are....

When you hold back who you really are, we all miss out. So whether you are a pet nut like me or a wordsmith like Patsy Clairmont, whether you like high heels or flip-flops, be who you really are. You have a voice and a style that is all your own. It has been given to you by God so that through you, a unique picture of our Father is seen.

Sheila Walsh
I'm Not Wonder Woman

Encouragement

COMFORT

support

relief

blessing

cheer

hope

persuasion

vigor

INSPIRATION

laughter

Girl Talk

Most women…love to think out loud. This is what "girl talk" is all about. We want to process the information out in the atmosphere as we are forming our opinions. We never really know what it is we think until we hear ourselves say it. This is why we need girlfriends—good girlfriends. People who know an awful lot about us and continue to choose to love us in spite of it. I call these sorts of friends The Gravity and Helium Group. They give me gravity because they know my faults, my weaknesses, my issues, my stubbornness, and my weirdness. The fact that they possess this sort of knowledge keeps me grounded….

These are also the people who can take my flagging balloon and fill it up with encouragement to remind me that I have flown before, I was born to fly, and I will fly again. There is nothing like the encouragement of a true friend.

Anita Renfroe
The Purse-Driven Life

Whiners neither enjoy nor give joy.

But grace-filled people are reputable,

sought after, and deeply loved.

—Patsy Clairmont

To Love as Jesus Loves

Our entire purpose in life is to learn to
love as Jesus loves. And how does He love?
Unselfishly, constantly, deeply, purely,
generously. As long as we are in the human
condition, this will not be easy. Count on it.
There will be people who will get under our
skin so badly we'll want to throttle them, but
trust me on this—it is possible to love them.
Sometimes the difficulty of loving comes in
the tiniest ways—when people are petty or
aggravating or they interrupt your day or
they want more of you than you want to give.
That kind of behavior is a pain in the neck.
But we're commanded to love these people.
The only way we can do it is to ask God for
patience and kindness and then to believe
He gives it to us in order to reach out to others
with those two attributes under our belts.

Luci Swindoll

Life! Celebrate It

GRACE UNDER PRESSURE

God's blessings are dispensed
according to the riches of
His grace, not according to
the depth of our faith.

—Max Lucado

Tender Adjustments

Have you ever seen a cashew in its shell?
Me neither. It turns out that a cashew has
caustic oil between the nut's inner and outer
shells. To rid this delectable treat of its acerbic
element, the outer shell is burned or roasted
off, and then the nut is boiled or roasted again
to remove the inner shell.

Life's hardships often feel as though someone
has turned up the heat on us, and we wonder
if we'll survive. Yet I find when I've been
"roasted" long enough in life's difficulties,
my outer casing of bad attitudes, preconceived
notions, and high-mindedness is burned off.
I'm left meeker, less defensive, more pliable,
and less caustic.

Jesus died for every "nut" in the land…even
the hardest one. And for that, I'm
particularly grateful.

Patsy Clairmont
All Cracked Up

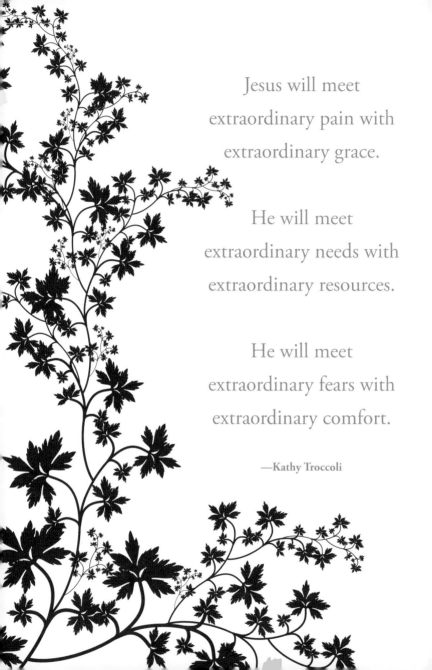

Jesus will meet
extraordinary pain with
extraordinary grace.

He will meet
extraordinary needs with
extraordinary resources.

He will meet
extraordinary fears with
extraordinary comfort.

—Kathy Troccoli

The Prescription for Worry

We can't add a minute to our life by worrying. Simply put, worry is useless. I am prone to worry somewhat about myself but endlessly over [my children]. All our worry in the name of love can accomplish absolutely nothing. But all our praying in the name of Jesus could entreat God to accomplish anything. When will we learn to turn our worry effort into prayer?

Christ's remedy for worry is to be like the ravens and lilies—trust God to do His job (Luke 12:25–26). The prescription for worry is trust. Trust comes to those who take God at His Word.

Beth Moore
Jesus, the One and Only

A Greater Purpose

Several weeks ago, I was hit with a
disappointment that took me by surprise.
I hurt and I ached, I prayed and I fussed,
and although I could manage a momentary
resolution, the unfairness of the situation
continued to torment me.

On one of the days during this mini-crisis,
I was reading one of my favorite devotional
authors, Amy Carmichael. Some words she
wrote grabbed my attention and I've been
holding on to them ever since:

NOTHING IS GOING WRONG
HOWEVER WRONG IT SEEMS.
ALL IS WELL.

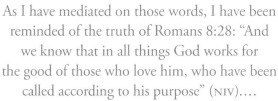

As I have mediated on those words, I have been reminded of the truth of Romans 8:28: "And we know that in all things God works for the good of those who love him, who have been called according to his purpose" (NIV)....

Has someone treated you unjustly?
God says, "Don't worry. I will make it work for your good."

Have you been passed over for a promotion?
God says, "Don't be anxious, I know all about it. I will use it for your growth and preparation for better things ahead."

Has someone hurt you deeply? God says, "Go ahead and cry. I know it hurts. But in the end your pain will serve a greater purpose."

Jan Silvious
The 5-Minute Devotional

Be anxious for nothing, but in everything by prayer and supplication, with thanksgiving, let your requests be made known to God; and the peace of God, which surpasses all understanding, will guard your hearts and minds through Christ Jesus.

Philippians 4:6–7

Thoughts of Peace

Girlfriend, the peace that surpasses all understanding is there for the asking! It's as near as your next breath. The next time your emotions threaten to spill over, the next time some fool is standin' on your last nerve, try to keep your wits about you long enough to breathe in a humble prayer, letting God know that you desperately need his help. (Of course he knows this already, but he loves to be asked.) By the time you let out that breath you can feel assured that he is making your request a priority and thinking thoughts of peace for you to keep your heart and mind from imploding.

Thelma Wells
The Buzz

In the middle of the muddle our
holy Lord is calmly at work.

—Elisabeth Elliot

Finding Grace to Help

Many years ago, we lost a baby girl. She was only fifteen days old. To this day, I feel a bond with women who have lost a baby. That woman knows my experience. I know her experience. I've been there. Scripture says Jesus has been there, too. He knows what you feel. If you are divorced and you know others in the Christian world who are divorced, you know the bond that grows when you talk to a woman whose husband left after twenty years of marriage. Through the sharing of the pain, the shock, and the rejection, you experience a bond. Scripture says Jesus did that, too. He has been where you and I have been, and because He's been there, He doesn't judge us in our weakness. He doesn't judge us when we're afraid. Instead, Scripture tells us to "come boldly to the throne of grace, that we may obtain mercy and find grace to help in time of need" (Hebrews 4:16).

Marilyn Meberg
Overcoming Difficulties

When the woman saw that she was
not hidden, she came trembling; and
falling down before [Jesus],
she declared to Him in the presence
of all the people the reason she had
touched Him and how she was
healed immediately.

And He said to her, "Daughter, be of
good cheer; your faith has made you
well. Go in peace."

Luke 8:47–48

Reaching Out to God

It's true that sometimes when we need Him most we feel far away from God—hurting, alone, forgotten, trampled down by a crowd of problems. Maybe at that point we've given up on ever feeling close to Him again. Maybe we feel dirty and unfit, covered with worldly dust that robs us of courage and weakens our faith.

Well, girlfriend, let me tell you: when you find yourself in that kind of ordeal, remember the woman in the Bible who reached out through the mob to touch the hem of Jesus' cloak. There may have been something in her that wanted to think He had passed her by or forgotten her or turned His back on her.…Ah, but she *knew* better. She knew that even if she didn't feel close to Jesus, even if she couldn't look Him in the eye and talk to Him face to face, *He* still knew she was there. So she came up behind Him and flung out her arm through the raucous crowd, knowing,

If I only touch His cloak, I will be healed.

And she did. And she was.

Thelma Wells
What These Girls Knew

A Grateful Heart

I believe the key to celebration is a grateful
heart, which means we search daily for reasons
to stand up and shout, "Let's party!"

Here's a gratitude jump-start list:

- Bumping into an old friend
- Raindrops on petals
- A child's giggle
- A yummy book
- Meaningful conversation
- Shared laughter
- Sweet dreams
- Soft pillows
- Starlit nights

Now join in and extend the list to include
all the marvelous reasons you have to
be upbeat and confetti-ready. Celebrate,
girlfriend! Celebrate!

Patsy Clairmont
Contagious Joy

What's on your gratitude list?

_____
_____
_____
_____
_____
_____
_____
_____

"Trading Places" Prayer

Sometimes, when I pray, I can't
see the forest for the trees.…
Drowning in the sea of my
own problems, I feel like I'm
flailing and grasping, tossed
by the waves.…

That's when I shift my prayers to
someone else.…

I remember unloading my
frustrations on my friend Karen
while we talked on the phone
one day. Sometimes [being blind]
just scrapes against the bottom
of my soul and makes me tired,
and it was one of those days.
My thoughts were fragmented,
and I was so overwhelmed by
circumstances that I could barely
articulate my heart.

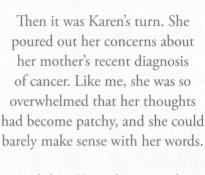

Then it was Karen's turn. She poured out her concerns about her mother's recent diagnosis of cancer. Like me, she was so overwhelmed that her thoughts had become patchy, and she could barely make sense with her words.

And then Karen hit upon the solution. "I know!" she said. "I'll pray for you today, and you pray for me. I can handle praying for your situation much better than I can figure out how to pray for mine."

On that day of "trading places" prayer, I didn't feel empowered because my own circumstances had changed. Somehow, God's grace and power swept through me as I poured myself out for Karen.

Jennifer Rothschild
Lessons I Learned in the Light

Our Devoted Father

God is not wringing His hands and fretting
about our mindlessness as we veer
repeatedly off the path He has determined
for our future….

Sooner or later, the Father knows His child
will act upon the inner nudge to call home.
When we find ourselves lost and in despair the
Father promises that when we call,
He'll answer. He will also listen.

In the listening, He will not respond with
words that condemn us, belittle us, or reject
us. In fact, on the contrary, the Father doesn't
even ask for an explanation. He asks only that
we come home.

Marilyn Meberg
Women of Faith Devotional Bible

I know the thoughts that I think
toward you, says the LORD,
thoughts of peace and not of evil,
to give you a future and a hope.

Jeremiah 29:11

GOD'S GREAT GRACE

My favorite thing
that God gives is
grace.
It is without
performance, free
in Christ.

—Luci Swindoll

God's Good Graces

Let's face it: we're going to mess up
occasionally; it's just part of our weakness as
human beings. But the Bible says when we
need forgiveness we should "come boldly
to the throne of grace, that we may obtain
mercy and find grace to help in time of need"
(Hebrews 4:16).

Imagine that! When we make a mistake,
we aren't expected to grovel our way back
into God's good graces. We're privileged to
march up to His throne of grace boldly, not
hanging back, not whimpering and whining,
but boldly coming before Him to "obtain
mercy and find grace." Is our God a great
God, or what?!

Thelma Wells
Listen Up, Honey

Traveling Free and Light

I wish I were better at the packing/traveling-light
gig. I think it's my insecurities that keep me
piling the stuff in. Will I have enough? Have
I covered every eventuality? Will I be caught
without something I really need? Will there be
a 24-Hour Super Target where I'm going?

And my life is like that. I spend too much
time accumulating stuff that is supposed

to ward off regrets. Instead, it makes me a terribly encumbered traveler, ever hoisting my junk from one phase of life to the next. I'm not sure if it's more difficult to keep from acquiring too much stuff or to let go of the stuff I no longer need. And when it comes to emotional baggage, I think we all come with fully matched sets.

I love what Jesus said about traveling with Him: "Are you tired? Worn out?…Come to me. Get away with me and you'll recover your life. I'll show you how to take a real rest…. Keep company with me and you'll learn to live freely and lightly" (Matthew 11:28, MSG).

Freely and lightly—sounds like a great invitation to exchange the baggage carousel for the one that comes standard with music, pretty horses, and the wind in your face. No carry-ons allowed.

Anita Renfroe
The Purse-Driven Life

God has never taken His eyes off you. Not for a millisecond. He's always near. He lives to hear your heartbeat. He loves to hear your prayers. He'd die for your sin before He'd let you die in your sin, so He did.

—Max Lucado

You Are Precious to Him

God wants you to think that not only are you His dearly loved child, but He loves you with tender compassion. Psalm 103:13–14 (NIV) reads: "As a father has compassion on his children, so the LORD has compassion on those who [reverence] him."

Sweet baby, I suggest you close your eyes for a moment. See the image of Jesus blessing the children, tenderly placing His hands on their heads. Then see yourself as one of the children in that group of little ones surrounding Jesus. Feel His touch on your head. Rest in this image again and again, every day....You are precious to Him.

Marilyn Meberg
Since You Asked

You say, "I can't go on."

God says, "My grace is sufficient."

You say, "I can't do it."

God says, "You can do all things."

—Barbara Johnson

Let the Burdens Fall Off

"Commit your works to the Lord, and your thoughts will be established" (Proverbs 16:3).
The word *commit* in the context of this verse is very interesting. The Hebrew word is *galal.* It means, "To roll; roll away."

The word *galal* is used often to describe the way a camel gets rid of its burden. It is a two-step process. First, it kneels down, and then it rolls to the left and the load falls off its back. The picture for us is a beautiful one. We are invited to kneel before God but encouraged not to stop there. We are called to roll over and let the burdens fall off our backs. We are called to roll every burden, every concern for the future, onto the Lord, sure that He will accept that responsibility and will bless us. *Whatever you are facing right now, kneel before God and roll into His grace.* He wants to carry your burden. You don't have to carry it anymore.

Sheila Walsh
The Heartache No One Sees

Believing God truly cares
is worth a fortune
in hope, victory, and spiritual rest.

—Luci Swindoll

God Buys Back Our Messes

Marshall, a hairstylist friend, is a devoted Christian. Whenever he styles a woman's hair, he prays out loud before he begins. One day several years ago, just as he started to cut my hair, he prayed, "Thank you, God, that you are a Redeemer. Not only do you buy us back from the consequences of our sin, but you buy back our messes as well."

I can tell you that prayer gave me a start! I have to smile as I think of it now. Of course, I had no reason to fear. I loved the new hairstyle Marshall gave me, but more than that, he left me with a profound thought as well: We have a God who buys back our messes!

God really does buy back our messes, and He buys them back whether we have blown it or whether it is someone else who has messed up our lives.

Jan Silvious
The 5-Minute Devotional

God Is Really God!

A friend of mine read the entire Bible when she was twelve. When she finished, she said to her mother, "Wow! God is really, really God." What a statement! My little friend understood that God is powerful and accomplishes His purposes even when it makes no sense to us. He is strong and good, whether we recognize it or not.

And He is God. He's not afraid of being misunderstood by anyone. He always does what is right, in order to fulfill His purpose. The strength of that and His absolute sovereignty give me security. He is really, really God.

Mary Graham
Women of Faith Devotional Bible

Stepping Out of Life's Routine

How sad for us when we are caught in the tension of our routine and miss the splendor of God's creation.

When was the last time you…

- Stared into the dazzling pattern of the stars?

- Gathered a fistful of lilies of the valley?

- Crammed a jar full of hydrangeas?

- Sat at the water's edge and leaned in to hear its song?

- Sifted sand through your toes?

- Traced the lines on a beautiful seashell?

- Introduced a child to a tadpole?

- Took a walk and listened to the songs of summer, autumn, winter, or spring?

Patsy Clairmont
All Cracked Up

*What fun and relaxing things
would you add to Patsy's list?*

_____

_____

_____

_____

_____

_____

_____

_____

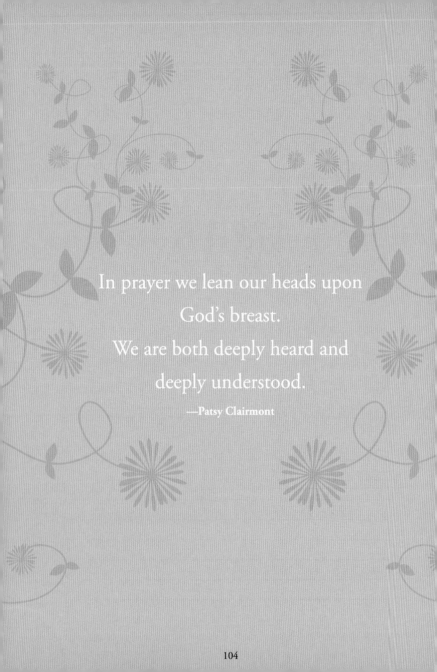

In prayer we lean our heads upon
God's breast.
We are both deeply heard and
deeply understood.

—**Patsy Clairmont**

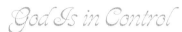

God Is in Control

One of the things I first noticed about control-top pantyhose is how great it is to take them off. What a relief! It's the same way with the tight control we try to have on our lives. If only we could grasp that…

God is in control, not your husband.

God is in control, not your children or parents.

God is in control, not your doctor.

God is in control, not your boss.

God is in control, not a terrorist.

No matter what is going on in your life right now, God loves you and He is in control, so you don't have to be! Take those uncomfortable control-top hose off and breathe a sigh of relief.
You are a wonderful woman!

Sheila Walsh
I'm Not Wonder Woman

Nothing—*absolutely nothing*—in this entire world can separate us from the love of God.

—**Sheila Walsh**

God Is Full of Grace

I'm embarrassed at how often I've heard myself say, "Oh, God, *please*...." I learned to beg with my mother, so I employ those same techniques with God. To my relief, it never works.

You see, God's Word says He is a sun and a shield. A sun provides light so we can see. And a shield protects us from what we can't see. He has the grace to give us both.

I've learned God is *full* of grace. He withholds nothing that is good for me. I walk with Him; He shows me the way. I have a need; He provides it. When it isn't the fulfillment of my own imaginings, I trust Him. He sees the end from the beginning. He has the grace to give me what I need, and the grace to not. He's *full* of grace.

Mary Graham
Women of Faith Devotional Bible

Let us therefore come boldly to the
throne of grace,
that we may obtain mercy and find
grace to help in time of need.

Hebrews 4:16

Wrapped in God's Love

You don't have to wait until your emotions are
in check before you come to Jesus. He wants
us to come as we are, broken and bruised with
tear-stained faces. We bring together all that is
true about us and all that is true about God.

We are invited to come right now as we are,
ragged at the edges, splattered by the mud of
life, invited into the very heart of heaven, and
called to move close and approach the throne
of grace. You don't have to tidy yourself up,
clean up your own mess, or wait till you feel
holy. Just come now into His presence. Jesus
sees your pain and longs to comfort you. As
my friend Barbara Johnson says, "Let God
wrap you in His comfort blanket of love."

Sheila Walsh
The Heartache No One Sees

You will never go where God is not. You may be transferred, enlisted, commissioned, reassigned, or hospitalized, but—brand this truth on your heart—you can never go where God is not.

— Max Lucado

Acknowledgments

Grateful acknowledgment is made to the following publishers for permission to reprint this copyrighted material.

Carolyn Arends ©, *Living the Questions* (Eugene: Harvest House, 2000)

Patsy Clairmont ©, *The Hat Box* (Nashville: W. Publishing Group, 2003)

Patsy Clairmont ©, *All Cracked Up* (Nashville: Thomas Nelson, Inc., 2006)

Patsy Clairmont et al. ©, *The Great Adventure* (Nashville: W. Publishing Group, 2002)

Henry Cloud ©, *Changes that Heal* (Grand Rapids: Zondervan, 1990)

Carol Kent ©, *Tame Your Fears* (Colorado Springs: NavPress, 1993)

Marilyn Meberg ©, *I'd Rather Be Laughing* (Nashville: W. Publishing Group, 1998)

Marilyn Meberg ©, *The Zippered Heart* (Nashville: W. Publishing Group, 2001)

Marilyn Meberg ©, *Overcoming Difficulties* (Nashville: Thomas Nelson, Inc., 2004)

Marilyn Meberg ©, *Since You Asked* (Nashville: W. Publishing Group, 2006)

Beth Moore ©, *Jesus, the One and Only* (Nashville: Broadman and Holman, 2002)

Chonda Pierce ©, *Roadkill on the Highway to Heaven* (Grand Rapids: Zondervan, 2006)

Anita Renfroe ©, *The Purse-Driven Life* (Colorado Springs: NavPress, 2005)

Anita Renfroe ©, *If It's Not One Thing It's Your Mother* (Colorado Springs: NavPress, 2006)

Jennifer Rothschild ©, *Lessons I Learned in the Light* (Colorado Springs: Multnomah Publishers, Inc., 2006)

Jan Silvious ©, *Big Girls Don't Whine* (Nashville: W. Publishing Group, 2003)

Jan Silvious ©, *The 5-Minute Devotional* (Grand Rapids: Zondervan, 1991)

Luci Swindoll ©, *I Married Adventure* (Nashville: W. Publishing Group, 2002)

Luci Swindoll ©, *Life! Celebrate It* (Nashville: W. Publishing Group, 2006)

Sheila Walsh ©, *The Heartache No One Sees* (Nashville: Thomas Nelson, Inc., 2004)

Sheila Walsh ©, *I'm Not Wonder Woman* (Nashville: Thomas Nelson, Inc., 2006)

Sheila Walsh ©, *Extraordinary Faith* (Nashville: Thomas Nelson, Inc., 2005)

Thelma Wells ©, *The Buzz* (Nashville: W Publishing Group, 2000)

Thelma Wells ©, *Listen Up, Honey* (Nashville: W Publishing Group, 2004)

Thelma Wells ©, *What These Girls Knew* (Nashville: W Publishing Group, 2007)

Women of Faith ©, *Women of Faith Devotional Bible* (Nashville: Thomas Nelson Bibles, 2003)

Women of Faith ©, *Contagious Joy* (Nashville: W. Publishing Group, 2006)

Other Books by Women of Faith

Irrepressible Hope
Faith for a Lifetime
Contagious Joy
Amazing Freedom

By Patsy Clairmont

All Cracked Up
Dancing Bones
I Second that Emotion

By Marilyn Meberg

God at Your Wit's End
Free Inside and Out
Love Me, Never Leave Me

By Luci Swindoll

Notes to a Working Woman
Life! Celebrate It!
Free Inside and Out

By Sheila Walsh

I'm Not Wonder Woman
God Has a Dream for Your Life
Get Off Your Knees and Pray

By Thelma Wells

The Buzz
Listen Up, Honey
What These Girls Knew

Notes

Notes